The Compost Heap

Sharon Katz Cooper

Chicago, Illinois

www.heinemannraintree.com
Visit our website to find out more information about Heinemann-Raintree books.

To order:

☎ Phone 888-454-2279
💻 Visit www.heinemannraintree.com
to browse our catalog and order online.

Edited by Charlotte Guillain, Rebecca Rissman, and Sian Smith
Designed by Joanna Hinton-Malivoire
Picture research by Tracy Cummins and Heather Mauldin
Originated by Chroma Graphics (Overseas) Pte. Ltd
Printed and bound in China by Leo Paper Products

14 13 12 11 10
10 9 8 7 6 5 4 3 2 1

Library of Congress Cataloging-in-Publication Data
Katz Cooper, Sharon.
The compost heap / Sharon Katz Cooper.
 p. cm. -- (Horrible habitats)
Includes bibliographical references and index.
ISBN 978-1-4109-3495-6 (hc)
ISBN 978-1-4109-3503-8 (pb)
1. Urban ecology (Biology)--Juvenile literature. 2. Compost animals--Habitat--Juvenile literature. 3. Compost--Juvenile literature. I. Title.
QH541.5.C6K382 2009
577.5'6--dc22
                                        2009002910

Acknowledgments

The author and publisher are grateful to the following for permission to reproduce copyright material: Age Fotostock p. **29** (© ARCO/J Meul); Alamy pp. **7** (© Kathy deWitt), **10** (© Mark Boulton), **12** (© Mediacolors), **15** (© Graham Corney), **19** (© David Chapman); Ardea pp. **22** (© John Mason), **23** (© Mark Boulton); Dwight Kuhn Photography p. **24** (© Dwight Kuhn); Getty Images pp. **5** (© Roine Magnusson), **6** (© Xavier Bonghi), **18** (© DEA/Christian Ricci); Minden p. **25** (© Mitsuhiko Imamori); National Geographic Stock p. **27** (© Kim Wolhuter); Photolibrary pp. **9** (© Andrea Jones), **20** (Bildagentur RM); Photoresearchers, Inc. pp. **13** (© SciMAT), **16** (© SPL); Photoshot p. **14** (© Bruce Coleman Inc/Bartomeu Borrell); Shutterstock pp. **4** (© Steve Byland), **8** (© Colour), **11** (© Shutterlist), **21** (© ENOXH), **26** (© Dr. Morley Read); Visuals Unlimited, Inc. p. **17** (© Nigel Cattlin).

Cover photograph of kitchen waste reproduced with permission of Photoresearchers, Inc. (© Mark Boulton).

Every effort has been made to contact copyright holders of any material reproduced in this book. Any omissions will be rectified in subsequent printings if notice is given to the publisher.

All the Internet addresses (URLs) given in this book were valid at the time of going to press. However, due to the dynamic nature of the Internet, some addresses may have changed, or sites may have changed or ceased to exist since publication. While the author and publisher regret any inconvenience this may cause readers, no responsibility for any such changes can be accepted by either the author or the publisher.

Some words are shown in bold, **like this**. You can find out what they mean by looking in the glossary.

Contents

What Is a Habitat?

A **habitat** is a place where plants and animals can get what they need to live. What do they need? Like you, they need food, water, and shelter.

woodpecker

4

5

rotting food

Did you know your leftover food could be used again? A compost heap is a pile of rotting food. This pile of rotting food is a **habitat** too!

A compost heap is made of fruit and vegetable scraps. You might also find old newspaper, leaves, and dead plants there. They are all slowly rotting. The living things in the compost heap turn it all into fresh soil!

This moldy banana is slowly rotting.

Compost heaps must be dark, warm, and a little bit wet. That is the best **habitat** for the animals and tiny living things who turn the food scraps into soil. The tiny living things are called **microbes**.

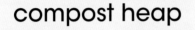

compost heap

eggshell

tea bag

banana peel

11

These apples are starting to rot, or break down.

12

This is a photo of bacteria seen through a microscope.

Bacteria are a **microbe.** They are so small you can only see them through a microscope. **Fungi** are also microbes. Bacteria and fungi get to work first. They begin breaking down food scraps into smaller pieces.

13

Here Come the Worms!

Worms are the superstars of a compost **habitat**! You can find worms in many compost heaps. They eat the rotting food. Then the worms poo out rich soil.

FUN FACT

If a worm's skin dries out it will die because a worm breathes through its skin.

Worms have many **segments**, or parts. Some of the segments have tiny stiff hairs. Worms use these hairs to help them move.

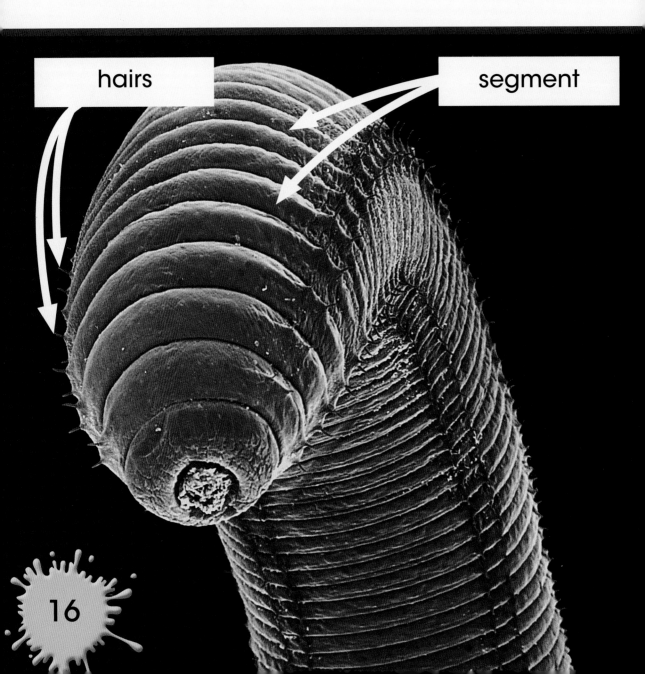

hairs

segment

Except for those hairs, worms have nothing else sticking out from their bodies. This long, smooth shape helps them **burrow** or dig down into the compost.

mucus

18

Worms make a lot of slippery **mucus** on their skins. Mucus covers their bodies. It keeps them wet and helps them to slide through food scraps and soil.

FUN FACT

Worms have no eyes but can still sense light and will move away from it.

Squirming and Sucking

Compost worms squirm through food scraps. They suck up rotting food. Strong muscles in the worms' gut mix up food with **digestive juices**. This breaks down the food into smaller and smaller bits.

These worms are busy
eating rotting food.

Worms poo out little piles of partly digested food. Believe it or not, these piles make great soil. It is perfect as **fertilizer**, which is something used to help plants grow.

FUN FACT

Earthworm poo piles are called **casts**.

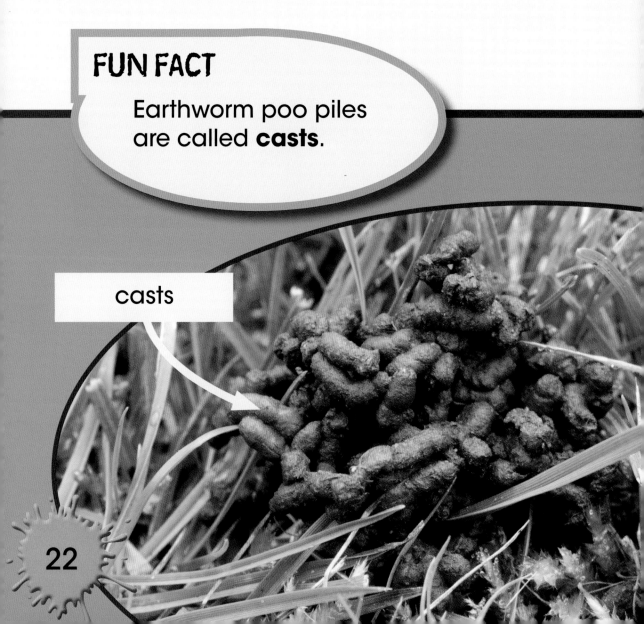

casts

Earthworm poo is rich in **nutrients**.
Nutrients are things plants need
to help them grow.

23

Plopping Pill Bugs

Worms are not the only animals in the compost heap. There are also lots of pill bugs. These little creatures chew up dead plants. They leave behind little pellets of poo. The pellets are full of **nutrients** for good soil.

pill bug

pill bug poo

25

Vomiting Flies

Flies also like to feed on rotting fruits and vegetables. They vomit on their food before they eat it. The vomit helps to break down the food. Then they can slurp it up with their tongues.

Watch a Worm

What you need:
- a place with earthworms
- gardening gloves (if you'd like to use these)
- your eyes

What to do:

1. Find a good outdoor place with soil and earthworms in it.

2. Dig around a little bit with your hands to break up the soil. Dig until you bring up some worms.

3. Choose one or two worms and watch them for a while.

4. What do you see them do? How do they move? Do you see them eating? How do they do it?

Glossary

bacteria type of tiny living thing you can see only through a microscope

burrow to dig in

casts piles of worm poo

digestive juices liquids in the stomach that help break down food

fertilizer something that helps make soil better for growing things in

fungi plant-like living things like mushrooms

habitat place where animals and plants live and grow

microbes tiny living things you can see only through a microscope

mucus slippery slime produced by some animals. Humans make mucus too.

nutrients something that plants and animals need to be healthy

segment section or part

Find Out More

Find out

How many hearts does a worm have?

Books to Read

Chappell, Rachel. *What's Going on in the Compost Pile? A Book About Systems.* Vero Beach, FL: Rourke Publishing, 2008.

Pfeffer, Wendy. *Wiggling Worms at Work.* New York: HarperCollins, 2003.

Websites

http://home.howstuffworks.com/composting.htm
This Website will help you learn more about how composting works.

http://sustainable.tamu.edu/slidesets/ kidscompost/kid1.html
This Website slide show will teach you how to make your own compost pile.

http://yucky.discovery.com/flash/worm/ pg000102.html
You can learn all about worms on this Website.

Index